Disappointed
But Not
Discouraged!!!

Sandra B. Randolph

LifeSkill® Institute, Inc.
P.O. Box 302
Wilmington, NC 28402

Published by: LifeSkill® Institute, Inc. SAN: 255-8440

Sandra B. Randolph, P.O. Box 847 Wilmington, NC 28402

Library of Congress Cataloging-in-Publication Data

Randolph, Sandra B. 1955—
        Disappointed But Not Discouraged!!!
        by Sandra B. Randolph
        ISBN   978-1-890199-12-8   paperback edition

Library of Congress Control Number:

        1. Religion I. Title II. Randolph, Sandra B.
        2. Psychology
        3. Death and Dying
        4. Christian Life
        5. Spiritual Growth

Printed in the United States of America

Publisher:
Lifeskill Institute Inc. SAN: 255-8440

P.O. Box 302
Wilmington, NC 28402
(800) 570-4009
Email: srandolph801@hotmail.com

Dedication

I dedicate this book to all who have had a loved one go to be with the Lord and are feeling guilty about not spending enough time with them or saying I should have, could have, but I did not.

Reading my book will encourage you to help someone else realize that you can be disappointed but not discouraged after understanding where their loved one is and that they are no longer suffering.

Table of Contents

Introduction

This book is about how I learned, after many years of family and friends dying, to be disappointed but not discouraged. Disappointed because they died but not discouraged if they had a relationship with the Lord. They are no longer suffering but are at peace with our Lord and Savior, Jesus the Christ.

This book was written for Christians, non-Christians, or anyone who will be faced with the death of a loved one, and they thought they understood the stages of death and dying. I personally went through three (3) stages.

The first stage is wanting to join the loved one in the casket, the second stage is accepting that they are gone and never coming back, and the final stage is that I have accepted the fact that my loved one is no longer suffering and they have received their healing.

After reading my story, you will have a deeper understanding of why you were disappointed that your loved one died. Still, you are not discouraged because you know where they are.

Disappointed But Not Discouraged!!!

Aunt Jeanette's Funeral

Saturday, September 22, 2018 – 11:00 a.m.

Let us pray. Father, in the name of Jesus, we come to you today, asking for strength as we go through this journey. Please help us to keep you first in our lives even as we go through this. Strip me of myself right now, and you come in the form of the Holy Ghost to say what needs to be said and to do what needs to be done. We decree it in the name of Jesus. Amen.

We acknowledge God the Father, Jesus, His son, and the Holy Spirit, our comforter. A special thanks to my cousin, Serena, for allowing me this opportunity to speak at the homegoing service of her mother, my aunt, Mrs. Jeanette Farmer Mapson.

I honor my husband, Apostle Ricky Randolph, and my brother, Dr. Gary Burns, who shares this pulpit with me. I also honor each of you who thought it not robbery to come to Virginia to support our family.

My scripture comes from John 14:1-6 – and it reads as follows:

1 – Let not your heart be troubled: ye believe in God, believe also in me.

2 – In my Father's house are many mansions: if it were not so, I would have told you.

3 – And if I prepare a place for you, I will come again, and receive you unto myself; that where I am, there ye may be also.

4 – And whither I go ye know, and the way ye know.

My subject today is – **Disappointed but not Discouraged!!!**

Let me define Disappointed: a feeling of dissatisfaction that follows the failure of expectations or hope to manifest something.

For example – you tried for years to get pregnant. You finally get pregnant, and your pregnancy ends in a miscarriage. Certainly, you are disappointed.

Earlier this month, I released a book entitled – **Pushing the Rock**. A book signing was scheduled with everything lined up at our annual Women's Retreat in Myrtle Beach, South Carolina. At the last minute, I was told the books would not be delivered in time for the book signing. Yes, I was disappointed.

This experience was an example of taking lemons and making lemonade. Therefore, what we did next was address labels and give a special on the books to whoever paid. When the books came, they would be mailed to them. I sold over 50 books that day.

What does it mean to be Discouraged? It means having lost confidence or enthusiasm, disheartened.

Disappointed but not Discouraged!!!

Hurricane Florence started as a category 5 storm, and prayers were answered. By the time it hit Wilmington, North Carolina, it was a category 2. We had five (5) days with no lights but some storm damage.

Actually, it was Hurricane Florence that kept us from getting to this service last week.

Disappointed but not Discouraged!!!

John 14:1 states *Let not your heart be troubled: ye believe in God, believe also in me.*

Point #1 – I was **disappointed** that Aunt Jeanette went home to be with the Lord on Tuesday, September 4, 2018.

Point #2 – I was **not discouraged** because she was a believer, accepted the Lord Jesus as her Lord and Savior, and is with Him now.

Point #3 – I was **disappointed** because she didn't beat cancer here on earth like she had done in the past.

Point #4 – I was **not discouraged** because the scripture declares in Isaiah 53:3 - "But he was wounded for our transgressions, he was bruised for our iniquities; the chastisement of our peace was upon him: and with his stripes we are healed."

I Peter 2:21 states *Who his own self bare our sins in his own body on the tree, that we, being dead to sins, should live unto righteousness; by whose stripes ye were healed.*

John 14:2 states *In my Father's house are many mansions: if it were not so, I would have told you. I go to prepare a place for you.*

Point #5 - I was **disappointed** because I didn't get to kiss her goodbye or build her a mansion here on earth.

Point #6 – I am **not discouraged** because she now has a mansion in my Father's house.

Point #7 – I was **disappointed** because she didn't answer the phone the last time I called.

Point #8 – **Not discouraged** because she answered the Father's call, and He welcomed her home.

Disappointed but not Discouraged

To our family, be encouraged, and let's strive to meet her again in the sweet by and by.

This sermon impressed upon my heart the desire to write a book dealing with death and dying.

Have you ever been **disappointed** about a situation that you had no control over? The first thing that comes to my mind is **death**. The only way that you can escape dying is not to be born. Over the years, I have personally encountered close friends and relatives who died - some old, some young. Some have lived a full life; some lives were cut short, either by an auto accident or sickness.

Disappointed but Not Discouraged Notes

_____

_____

_____

_____

_____

_____

_____

_____

_____

_____

_____

_____

_____

_____

_____

_____

_____

_____

_____

Remembering Grandma Lizzy
October 26, 1984

The earliest death that I remember that left an impact on me was my grandmother, Elizabeth Everett Mapson, aka Grandma Lizzie.

"Disappointed but Not Discouraged"

Thinking back on my time with my grandmother, I remember that she had a spirit of fear like no one else. She was a loving, kind, and understanding person, but she never wanted to be alone.

II Timothy 1:7 – *For God has not given us the spirit of fear; but of power, and of love, and of a sound mind.*

We tend to quote the scriptures over and over, but to have that scripture become real to us is a different story.

Spending time with my grandmother was the beginning of my reflexology ministry.

I remember spending a lot of time with my grandmother, especially on the weekends. She would allow me to comb and straighten her hair **(even though it didn't need it),** wash her feet **(prepared me for my foot ministry/ reflexology),** and even do her nails. She was my personal Real Barbie Doll.

My grandmother taught me what to do in the midst of a physical storm. We would lie across her bed, be quiet, and look out the window. When the lights went out, she would light the lantern for us to see. Those were good times and good days.

Disappointments in my life

I became pregnant out of wedlock at the age of nineteen (19). My grandmother never condemned me. As a matter of fact, she said, "You and the baby can come and spend the night with me."

One incident happened when Ulric (my oldest son) got sick at my grandmother's house. His fever went up too high too quickly, and it caused him to have a seizure. We called 911 and looking back on the incident; I could see fear in her eyes. Ulric was taken to the hospital, where he was admitted.

He was very sickly in his younger years, so much so until we were one of the last patients at Babies Hospital in Wrightsville Beach, North Carolina before they closed. From that moment on, she never asked us to spend the night again.

I worked at E.I. Dupont in Leland, North Carolina, and made a decent salary. There was nothing that I would not do for my grandmother. I made sure all of her church dues were paid in a timely manner. Everyone knew how I felt about my grandmother.

I remember my cousin, Fennell, saying that when it came time to vote for the Pastor, he told my grandmother she had to do what I said because I paid her general claims. Back in the day, for you to vote whether you wanted the Pastor to stay or go, your general claims had to be paid in full. My job at E.I. Dupont afforded me the opportunity to have her general claims paid.

She was my heart. I remember the week of her death. She was no longer afraid to die. She made her peace with the Lord, and He welcomed her home to her mansion.

October 26, 1984, was her date of death, according to the death records of the Brunswick County Register of Deeds Office. I was twenty-nine years old. Her funeral was at Johnson Chapel A.M.E. Zion Church in Leland, North Carolina. I still remember screaming and howling uncontrollably, looking in her casket.

Disappointed but Not Discouraged

Someone came and got me from the casket and told me to let her go. I really didn't understand what they meant.

Time to let go

Even though I was twenty-nine years old, I still did not have a complete understanding of death. It took me years later to come to the full knowledge of what death meant.

I kept saying a part of me died with her. Still crying uncontrollably, I kept confessing that you don't understand; a part of me died as well. I started getting sick when I made that statement and did not know why.

In our ignorance, we say things and don't realize our words are very powerful. We can speak things into existence. Well, I did. Doctor visit after doctor visit, I finally realized that I had released into the atmosphere that a part of me died when my grandmother died. Therefore, I had to go back and snatch those words out of the atmosphere and release healing in the name of Jesus instead.

Death and life in the power of your tongue

Proverbs 18:21 – *Death and life are in the power of the tongue: and they that love it shall eat the fruit thereof.*

From that point on, I had to start confessing healing scriptures.

Psalms 118:17 – *I shall not die, but live, and declare the works of the Lord. Isaiah 53:5 – But he was wounded for our transgressions, he was bruised for our iniquities: the chastisement of our peace was upon him; and with his stripes we are healed.*

Over and over, I started confessing these scriptures over my life. I had to realize that my grandmother was with the Lord, and if I also wanted to be with Him, I had to live the life that she lived to get my reward.

I was only twenty-nine years old. No way was I going to die prematurely. My health seemed to change when I changed my diet, of what I was eating, physically and spiritually. My words changed from death to life. My confession was from that point, "I am going to be one hundred and fifty-five (155) years old when I die." I told all that knew me that if I was pronounced dead and I was not one hundred and fifty-five years old (155), somebody better begin to pray and call me back.

I loved my grandmother, but she was now resting in the bosom of our Lord and Savior.

I was disappointed but not discouraged.

Disappointed but Not Discouraged Notes

_____

_____

_____

_____

_____

_____

_____

_____

_____

_____

_____

_____

_____

_____

_____

_____

_____

_____

_____

Vernie (my best friend)

Life was as normal as it could be, as I remembered. Then it started again. On April 7, 1990, my best friend, Janice Bryant (Vernie), died.

Vernie was the oldest sister of Cleo Willis, my classmate. She moved back to Wilmington from New Jersey, right down the street from me. Cleo contacted me and told me that she moved near me. We hit it off right away. She was older and taught me so much. It was Vernie who introduced me to theater and the arts. I saw my first play at Thalian Hall with her and her daughters (LaSabra and Deniel).

She joined the Naval Reserves, and I would help her train. Again, it was Vernie who got me into jogging. We even walked the lake weekly. We did everything together. She taught me how to cook different things. Just everything. We shared secrets. Yes, she was my best friend.

Disappointed but Not Discouraged

She was having some health problems and was excited because the doctors finally knew what was wrong with her.

On the day of her surgery, I was scheduled for a DNC (gynecological procedure). I told her I would come and see her as soon as I got myself together. Her daughter, LaSabra, called me to inform me of the results of her surgery.

She explained to me that when the doctors did the surgery, they opened her up and discovered that she had a rare form of liver cancer and was given the diagnosis that she would probably live two to four months. I asked her who she was talking about. She said, "Mommy." Wait, wait, what are you talking about? I could not believe what I was hearing. Vernie lived two days short of the diagnosis of two months.

Who Is Going To Be Strong for Me?

The day of her funeral, I was crying, and my mom came up to me and said, "Stop that crying. You need to be strong for her children." Yes, she had two daughters who no longer had a mother, but I no longer had my best friend. I stopped crying to help her daughters grieve.

Now, **who is going to be strong for me?** I was hurting as well. It was the worst thing my mom could have done. Exactly one year later, I was crying uncontrollably in my office at the Register of Deeds office, and I did not know why. While I was in the office crying, Michael Holden (another friend) was sent to my office to console me.

I had been talking to Michael about salvation because he had asthma, really bad. I told him, Michael, you need to be saved because, with your asthma, as bad as it is, you need Jesus. As I was crying, he asked me if my friend was saved. I said, "yes". He said, "Well, she is with the Lord." Immediately, my tears stopped. Weeks later, Michael came to me and told me I did not have to worry about him anymore. I asked him what he was talking about. He said he had a conversation with Jesus and received salvation. Talking about rejoicing. I rejoiced with him.

Disappointed but Not Discouraged

Ecclesiastes 3:1-11 - *To every thing there is a season, and a time to every purpose under the heaven:*

2 - *A time to be born, and a time to die; a time to plant, and a time to pluck up that which is planted;*

3 - *A time to kill, and a time to heal; a time to break down, and a time to build up;*

4 - *A time to weep, and a time to laugh; a time to mourn, and a time to dance;*

5 - *A time to cast away stones, and a time to gather stones together; a time to embrace, and a time to refrain from embracing;*

6 - A time to get, and a time to lose; a time to keep, and a time to cast away;

7 - A time to rend, and a time to sew; a time to keep silence, and a time to speak;

8 - A time to love, and a time to hate; a time of war, and a time of peace.

9 - What profit hath he that worketh in that wherein he laboureth?

10 - I have seen the travail, which God hath given to the sons of men to be exercised in it.

11 - He hath made every thing beautiful in his time: also he hath set the world in their heart, so that no man can find out the work that God maketh from the beginning to the end.

You see, my mom stopped my grief process when Vernie died, but there was purpose in what she did out of ignorance. I encourage everyone who has suffered the death of a loved one to grieve.

Ecclesiastes 3:4 -states – a time to weep, and a time to laugh; a time to mourn, and a time to dance.

When we do not mourn, grief comes out in some other form. See, I learned from my grandmother's death not to say a part of me died when Vernie died. I did not want to get sick again and not know why.

Reminder – Psalms 118:17 – I shall not die, but live and declare the works of the Lord.

Again, I was **disappointed but not discouraged** when Vernie died because she did not have to suffer any longer.

Disappointed but Not Discouraged Notes

_____
_____
_____
_____
_____
_____
_____
_____
_____
_____
_____
_____
_____
_____
_____
_____
_____
_____
_____

Michael Holden Died

Michael Holden (I talked about him earlier) was a friend I treated as a son. We spent time together when he would come into our office at the Register of Deeds. Michael worked for the Tax Office.

When Vernie died, it was Michael who came into my office when I was crying and could not stop. He asked me if Vernie was saved. I told him yes, she was. He told me that I did not have to worry about her, right? My tears stopped.

It was not long after Vernie's death that Tammy Beasley rushed into my office and asked me if I heard about Michael. I said, 'heard what?" She said, "he died this morning." I ran out of my office crying. I got half of the way down the back hallway and remembered the conversation that Michael and I had when he told me that he was saved. My tears again ceased. Tammy apologized to me because she did not know that I was that close to Michael. I had a black and white polka dot dress that became my funeral dress. I even wore it to Michael's funeral.

Disappointed but Not Discouraged

Another friend is gone. I got to the point that I did not try to get close to anyone. When anyone tried to get close to me, I would reject them because I did not want them to die. It seemed to me that if you got close to me, you would die.

Healing in my hands

I had grown since my grandmother's death and was growing spiritually as well. God blessed me to have the gift of healing in my hands. Ok, Lord, why is everyone around me dying if I had the gift of healing?

At this point, I stopped saying that I had the gift of healing. The Lord and I had a conversation. He asked me why I was not walking in my healing anointing. I told Him all my friends were dying, and I could not save them. He told me that if He told me to tell them that they were healed and they died, then they could blame Him, not me.

WOW. I did not have to take the blame when I laid my healing hands on folk, and they did not get well. **I was not God.** I was just **His instrument.** From then on, I started walking back in the healing anointing God gave me.

Disappointed but Not Discouraged

Disappointed but Not Discouraged Notes

_____

_____

_____

_____

_____

_____

_____

_____

_____

_____

_____

_____

_____

_____

_____

_____

_____

_____

_____

Disappointed But Not Discouraged!!!

Remembering My Daddy

I was at the point where I hated funerals. My daddy (Deacon Alfred Burns) had type 2 diabetes for most of his adult life. He was the type of person who would not take care of himself. Eventually, he was placed on dialysis because of kidney failure.

Dad was a trooper. I remember the day he and I were on his front porch, and we had that talk that no one wanted to have with their parents. My father said that he had decided to give each one of his children what he wanted them to have while he was alive so there would be no fighting when he died.

Then he asked me what I wanted. Wow, "I said. What do you have?" I thought about it for a moment. To make him laugh, I told him, give me all your money. He looked at me seriously and said, "Well, you just lucked out because I do not have any money." I told him that I did not want anything from him. I then realized that he trusted me to do certain things. I kept saying why don't you let this one do that or that one do something else. He kept saying, "I want you to do it."

Spending Time with My Dad

For the last three months of his life, I spent every day with him. He was a resident at North Chase Nursing Facility. I would see him before I went to work at 8:00 a.m. and again after I got off at 5:00 p.m. I would generally stay until around 11:00 p.m. every night. This went on for three months. I literally gave up everything to make sure my **daddy** was taken care of.

At some point, his shunt for giving him dialysis stopped up for the second time. I was his attorney-in-fact, but I always discussed every decision I made with him first. I told him that the shunt stopped up again, and it would mean he would have to have two more surgeries. I told him we were going to take him off of dialysis, but if there was anything he wanted, to let me know.

Dad also had a feeding tube. He asked me, "Anything like what?" I said, "**Anything**." He told me, "I want to eat." I said, "You got it." I went to the nurse's station and told them my dad wanted to eat. The nurse was upset with me and called the doctor on me. She said if I fed him, the food would go into his lungs and kill him. I told her, "Excuse me, he is already dying."

The doctor told her to allow me to feed him but instruct me how to use the suction machine in case he started choking. The nurse brought him a tray with pureed turkey, dressing, and green peas. I fed him and told him to hold the food in his mouth long enough for his brain to tell his stomach that food was coming.

Dad held that first spoonful in his mouth and savored it. After eating about 3-4 spoons, I asked him if he had had enough. He said, **"Had enough?"** So, therefore, I fed him a few more spoonfuls before he started choking. He never asked for any more food. He was satisfied.

Two aides who worked the night shift told me they would take good care of my dad. They informed me that they were going to a church conference and would be off for a couple of days, but when they came back, they would make sure he was well taken care of. While they were off, Dad transitioned that Sunday morning.

Disappointed but not discouraged.

Friday before Dad died, my brother Gary came home because he lived in Maryland and told me to go home, explaining to me that Mom wanted to stay at the nursing home with him that night. I prayed and asked the Lord not to allow him to transition while she was there because she was so fearful.

I went home Friday night and did not wake up until 9:00 a.m. Saturday morning. I jumped up because I felt like I had overslept. I got up, dressed, and returned to the nursing home. I stayed there until Dad got his wings. On Saturday there were lots of visitors. All the grands came to see him.

Final Hours with Dad

Early Sunday morning, his best friend, Mr. King Moore, entered his room around 6:30 a.m. I was leaning over Dad's bed, crying. An angel, unsure who she was because I never looked up, came in and massaged my back while I was crying. Mr. Moore was also crying. He told me I needed to stop fretting because my dad would not want that. Looking back, I had to smile because Mr. Moore was also crying. Dad waited until Mr. Moore left, and then he got on the train and went to be with the Lord.

Dad Got His Wings/The Longest walk of my life.

Dad got his wings on Sunday, September 23, 2001, at 6:45 a.m. I was with him when he took his last breath. One breath, and he was in the presence of the Lord. That was the turning point for me about death and dying.

Disappointed but not discouraged.

No more suffering, no more dialysis, no more nursing homes, no more, no more - Dad was finally free. I walked to the nurse's station, which seemed like a mile away, to inform the nurse that I felt like Dad was gone. The nurse walked with me to check his vitals. She confirmed that Dad was gone. She informed the funeral home of his death, and I called my mom's house. Mom answered the phone. I asked to speak to Wayne. When he got on the phone, I informed him that it was over. The staff got his roommate up, dressed him, and placed him in the hall so the family could come and show their final respect.

Disappointed but Not Discouraged

Senator Luther Jordan (owner of Jordan Funeral Home) called to inform me that he sent someone to come and pick up the body. He told me that he was at my disposal and if I needed anything, just let him know.

Pre-Need already done.

Dad trusted me to take care of his final business. June 2001, to qualify him for medical benefits, I purchased a pre-need policy for him and Mom. It was one of the hardest things I ever had to do because Dad and Mom were still alive.

We, as Black Americans, feel that to prepare for the funeral while the person is alive is disrespectful. I literally had to sit down with the funeral director (Mr. William Boykins) and outline their funerals. I had to pick out the casket, purchase it, pay for programs, pay for the cars to be used, and even pay for death certificates while they were alive. It was hard, but after Dad transitioned, nothing had to be done. Everything was paid in full.

I strongly suggest that everyone get a pre-need; trust me, it makes life much easier. A pre-need gives the person an opportunity to think with a clear head about how much money they want to spend and what area to put their money in the ground without feeling pressured when their loved one dies.

Dad and Mom wanted everything done in one day. Years earlier, Dad had an aunt who died in New York.

Her wake and funeral service were done on the same day. Senator Jordan had just built a new funeral home, and he and my mom agreed that they wanted everything done at the funeral home when their time came.

The Funeral

After Dad's service, I felt like a load was lifted off of me. I had done all I knew to do to carry out his wishes. Mom sang a solo. Wayne did his Eulogy. Rick and I did a duet. The Lord gave me a song to sing months before his death. Rick added the music to the song.

I Am Healed

I am healed (repeat 7 times)
I am healed (repeat 7 times)

By His stripes, I am healed
By His stripes, I was healed
I am healed, healed, healed.

By His Power, I am healed
By His Power, I was healed
Healed, healed, healed.

From Oppression, depression, heartache and pain
I am healed, healed, healed.
I am healed (repeat 7 times)

No more hospitals; I'm healed
No more nursing homes; I'm healed
I am healed, healed, healed.

No Dialysis; I'm healed.
No more needles; I'm healed.

I am healed (repeat 7 times)

Penned by Dr. Sandra B. Randolph
June 21, 2001

Disappointed but Not Discouraged

Rick and I sang this song. I promised the Lord that I would never sing it again. Since that time, I have sung it over and over again, when He laid it on my heart to sing. There were so many people at Dad's funeral. Uncle Edward Mapson told me how worried he was about me. He also said, I did good.

Turning Point

Yes, this was the turning point in my life where I looked at death in a totally different light. Watching Dad go from labor to his reward warmed my heart. No more suffering. No more going to dialysis three times a week. No more needles because he was hard to stick. Free at last. Free at last. One breath and he was Free at last.

All I had to do was make sure he had a clean suit, underwear, socks, and a T-shirt. Dad had a pre-need done before his death. Again, I strongly suggest purchasing a pre-need policy, and when the time comes, and it will come, no one can feed on your emotions.

Disappointed but Not Discouraged

During the last three months of Dad's life, I learned a lot from him. I remember right before he died, I told him how he always took us to our destination an hour ahead of time. Dad was in the military, and he learned how to be on time and taught us the same principle: the importance of being on time. Dad stopped dying long enough to say, "No, I didn't." That was too funny to me. During that time, he even told me he loved me. I already knew he loved me, but it was never verbally expressed.

Well, I am again **disappointed but not discouraged** because Dad was gone, and I was going to miss him. It took me a while not to take the exit to the nursing home, and I had to recalculate my route - not just my route but my life.

Disappointed but Not Discouraged Notes

Disappointed But Not Discouraged!!!

Recalculating My Route and My Life

Birth of Uplifting Faith Ministries, Inc.

After everything was over, I checked into an Extended Stay Hotel for three days, asking the Lord what he would have me do next. When I checked in, I had with me a gallon of water, a notebook for instructions, and my bible. Speak, Lord, speak. Well, the Lord spoke. He said, **"You are so tired. You need to rest. I want you to get in that bed and rest."** I was obedient, and I slept for a day and a half.

When I arrived at the hotel, I looked in the mirror and did not recognize myself. My face was swollen, and I truly looked a mess. Nobody told me I looked bad. Nobody told me I needed to rest. Nobody said you cannot minister to anyone until you get some rest. This was another turning point in my life. It is ok to rest. It is ok to say no, I can't do that, or I can't come to your party. It is okay to say no. I am not praying for you because I need prayer myself. I learned how to say - a two-letter word that was very powerful.

I checked out of the Extended Stay Hotel Sunday morning and picked up our granddaughter, Brianna. We drove to Kinston, North Carolina. I had on a black suit with a wide-brim black hat. I was in disguise. I needed a word from the Lord. Looking for directions, Brianna and I visited Prophet Daniel Williams' church for service in Kinston, North Carolina.

You Can Run, but You Can't Hide.

Remember now, I was in disguise. Prophet Williams was greeting the people at the door. When he shook my hand, he said, **"Wilmington, right?"** But, I am in disguise. Yes Sir, "I said." "Well, welcome to our service today." Prophet Williams' whole sermon was directed at me. He talked about Rizpah and how she took her place on the rock of Gibeah and, for five months, watched the suspended bodies of her children to prevent them from being devoured by the beasts and birds of prey. (II Samuel 21:10) He really ministered that word. I went there so broken. He called me up after the service was over and ministered to me, I know, for about forty-five minutes. He even had his wife come and just hold me. He told me I was a type of Rizpah, and I came there today for directions. I left with a clear understanding as to where to go.

Brianna and I went back to Wilmington, North Carolina. I shared my instructions with my husband. We asked for a meeting with my Pastors – Drs. Theodore and Joyce I. Jones to inform them that we would be starting our own ministry. **Uplifting Faith Ministries, Inc.** was birthed in that Extended Stay Hotel. After meeting with the Apostles, they said they would have a service and help us launch our ministry.

They even released Elder Florence Wheeler and Elder Hazel Hewitt to help us get started. They stayed with us on alternating Sundays to help us get started.

Disappointed but Not Discouraged Notes

_____

_____

_____

_____

_____

_____

_____

_____

_____

_____

_____

_____

_____

_____

_____

_____

_____

_____

What Am I going to do with Mom?

My next situation was what would happen to Mom, now that Dad is gone. Lord knows I was not moving to Leland; she was so stubborn. Mom was not going to leave her home. She lived alone for a minute, then my son, Stretch moved in with her. She was in hog heaven. He took his dog, Maxx, who was a rottweiler. One thing about a rottweiler is they only listen to one person. That person was Stretch. Maxx would do stuff and would look at you as if to say, "Make me stop." Mom wanted to have company one day but did not know how Maxx would react. She told her friend that she would try to put him in the bedroom, and then she could visit. Mom says to Maxx, "Maxx, my friend wants to come over and visit me. Do you mind going into the bedroom?" Maxx gave her a look as if to say, you won't have any company today. Mom had to call her friend back to inform her that her grandson was not home, and she could not get his dog to go into the bedroom. Therefore, she didn't feel it was safe to visit.

Stretch had a hard time with Mom. One night, he had a dream. In the dream, the Lord showed him that Mom would always leave the dining room light on, and when he came home, he would cut it off. When she woke up in the middle of the night and saw the light was off, she felt safe because Stretch was now in the house with her. He woke up. Normally, Stretch would call Rick and ask him to interpret his dream. He called me and told me he had a dream, and the Lord had already shown him the interpretation. From then on, he would wait until Mom went to sleep; he would go to Leland, cut the lights off, and then return to our house before she woke up. Mom thought he was in the house when she woke up and saw the lights were out. Poor Mom never knew. Today, he claims he did not do that. He said he would leave early in the morning before she got up. Stretch stayed with Mom for a while. Janice would stay on the weekends.

Bridget Moves from Atlanta

One day, Bridget called me and asked if I could help her move back home from Atlanta, Georgia. WOW, I thought this was going to really help with mom. I got my team together, Deacon Hines, Prophetess Hines, and Prophetess Kwabena, and we planned a road trip. I rented a U-haul, and it was attached to the back of the van. Deacon Hines was always our driver. We drove to Atlanta to pick Bridget up. Upon arrival, we noticed that she was walking with a walker. She had MS. (Multiple Sclerosis). She did not have much to bring because she gave most of her stuff away. Well, we got the U-haul packed up and headed back to Leland, North Carolina. At first, she dealt with it well. She was using a walker.

After getting her settled in, we applied for her disability. She told me she had a friend in Atlanta who started the process, but when I applied for her, we saw that it never went through. It did not take as long as most disability cases I heard about. God did it on her behalf. Now she was home. At first, things were ok.

We opened a joint checking account, and I gave her a debit card. **(MISTAKE)** Bridget felt she could spend her money as long as she had checks and a debit card. One of her favorite pastimes was ordering items online. She loved the Genie bras. Every month, she ordered at least two of them. She started placing her account in overdraft status. She would have an MS episode and would have to be hospitalized for three days to get intense steroids through an IV. When she was in the hospital, Mom would stay with us. After years of fighting this crippling disease, she ended up in a nursing home. The problem came back as to what I would do with Mom. She was welcome to come and live with my husband and me, but we were never home during the day. Mom was extremely lonely.

For Bridget's last visit to the hospital, the social worker said she needed long-term nursing care.

Long-Term Nursing Care

Silver Stream was a newer facility, and she was approved for a bed there. She stayed there for around five years when her health declined. My brother, Gary, moved back from Maryland to be closer home to help care for Mom and Bridget. He moved to Garner, North Carolina, and would drive down twice a week to sit with Bridget at the nursing home. He would push her outside in the wheelchair, in the sun, which she looked forward to every week. Transportation was arranged to get her to church on Sundays. She came every Sunday that she could come until she was no longer able to sit in a wheelchair. She was declining in health and was no longer able to sit in a wheelchair. She was then placed in a Jenny Chair (chair on wheels). The transportation service took her to church one time in the Jenny Chair. Then, it refused to take her from that point on, stating that it was against their policies to transport her in anything other than a wheelchair. Afterwards, her health declined more.

Two of her friends from Atlanta, Georgia, came to visit after they heard that her health was declining. (Angela D. Worrell, whom Bridget always called "Scott" and Cindy McClemore), They spent a couple of days in town, enjoying being with her at the nursing home. Angela said, "I'll never forget that visit because Bridget told us, "Y'all my people, I don't trust everyone, I know y'all." They left her with gifts and lots of love and memories.

Disappointed but Not Discouraged

Bridget had another friend who lived in Wilmington, Gerrie, who would visit her regularly. She could tell when Bridget's health was declining. Bridget contacted Mercer, an infection. After recovering from it, I noticed she had short-term memory loss. I actually thought Bridget was pretending with the memory loss episode. She was a handful at that nursing home. All of the staff knew her well. An aide, Karon Quince, was excellent with her. When Karen worked, I did not have to worry about her.

After the short-term memory loss, she had swallowing issues. A swallowing test was done, and she failed it. All of her food had to be pureed. She literally stopped eating because she said the food looked like dodo. Wayne could get her to eat when she would refuse to eat for the aides. Her plate would always be clean after his visits.

Another good friend was Pastor Grayland Bryant. He also visited her a couple of times when he was in town. Man, when he would come, she would smile for days afterward.

While Bridget was in long-term care, now this time was for good; Mom would stay with us most of the time. After being in the long term, the question came up as to what to do with Mom.

Severe Ice Storm

Finally, after an ice storm that left Mom without lights, Fred took her to Aunt Jackie's house (her sister). Aunt Jackie had lights and a wood stove. Mom sat by that wood stove and refused to leave from that point on. Uncle Dule and Aunt Jackie welcomed her into their home unconditionally. She was so happy. I was pleased also because I was at my wit's end trying to figure out what to do with Mom.

She was burning over 100 gallons of gas every two weeks. The lady at the gas company showed us favor. I promised to pay the bill if she gave her the gas: nobody but God. Mom was finally warm. Not only was she warm, but Aunt Jackie had a lot of traffic coming and going all the time. Mom loved company. Everything worked out perfectly.

Bridget Finally Healed of MS

August 12, 2017, was our 22nd anniversary. Pastors Tony and Janice Jenkins from Atlanta, Georgia, invited us to go with them to Hawaii for a rest and relaxation mini vacation. We were excited, but I could not pack. I started seeing the signs.

Bridget had been on morphine for over a year, and she started talking crazy. She asked me, "How did you find me? I told her I was a Detective, and it wasn't hard to find her. She said, "You brought me some clothes too, and they are pretty." Wayne came down twice a week to give me a break, and I asked him if she was acting any different to him. He said she was talking out of her head. I asked the nurse if it was coming from the morphine. She informed me that it was a side effect. I instructed her to change the morphine to something else. They gave her Ativan instead. I watched her, and she was like a zombie after taking the Ativan.

I then told the nurse to put her back on morphine because I would rather see her talking out of her head than be like a zombie. She never bounced back. The nursing home at Silver Stream was short-staffed, so I called Hospices (Palliative Care) and asked them to re-evaluate her. She even started running a fever. The nurse at the nursing home took over an hour and a half to give her a suppository for the fever and never gave it to her. I called Palliative Care again and asked them to place her in their facility.

They placed her in the Lower Cape Fear Life Care Center in Wilmington, North Carolina.

I contacted our siblings. Janice came and helped me clean her room out at the nursing home.

Bridget was transported to Lower Cape Fear Life Care within a few hours. She got better care at their facility the week she was there than she received the entire time she spent at the nursing home.

Lower Cape Fear Life Care Center is a center that helps patients with an easier transition with different meds that help them cross over easily. The staff, including the nurses, the doctors, and the administration, were very nice to all of us. The doctor even prayed with us and explained where she was in her transition.

On Wednesday, August 16, 2017, Bridget got her wings. No more nursing homes, no more long trips to doctor appointments, no more dealing with the side effects of MS (Multiple Sclerosis). She is finally resting in peace.

Disappointed but Not Discouraged because we know where she is and is no longer in any pain.

At her funeral, Wayne did the Eulogy. Ricky did the prayer of comfort and sang a solo. Hilda (our niece) also sang a solo. I made remarks. In the remarks, I explained how Bridget trusted me.

When you are given Power of Attorney over a person, folk often think you are taking something from that person. She trusted me. Even in the end, she trusted me to make her final arrangements. I was disappointed but not discouraged because I knew where she was. She is finally resting in peace.

Disappointed but Not Discouraged

Disappointed but Not Discouraged Notes

_____

_____

_____

_____

_____

_____

_____

_____

_____

_____

_____

_____

_____

_____

_____

_____

_____

_____

_____

_____

Disappointed But Not Discouraged!!!

Mama Mary Lee Jenkins
(February 17, 1941 - March 9, 2014)

Mama Mary, as she was affectionally called by many, was an amazing woman of God. She had seven children that she gave birth to, but nine total that she raised. But she also had a lot of spiritual children.

Mama Mary and Papa Joe joined our ministry at Uplifting Faith. They really were a blessing. Papa Joe had a lot of spiritual gifts, but he called them the Gypsy curse. They both were amazing. She even had healing in her hands and could minister to many in the ministry.

They both were ordained Deacons and Deaconesses, and on certain Sundays, they had to minister the word. Mama Mary spoke one time and tore the church up. She would not speak any after that.

Usually, on Wednesdays, she would call me and say, "Pastor Sandra, don't cook today. Just stop by here and get you and Pastor Ricky a plate of food." She always told me how much she loved us.

Every Sunday evening, we (Mama Mary, Blue, Hines, and myself) would get on the phone and discuss who had torn up the church that day. We also would make plans for what we would do if we were ever rich.

March 14, 2014 – she passed at NHRMC. She got her reward. The whole family was devasted. To this date, they are still suffering from her leaving them. As much as she loved her family, I promise you, she would not come back here for nothing in the world. She is free and healed.

After writing the song, I Am Healed, she asked me to put it on a cassette tape for her. When she would get in her car, she would play that cassette. No matter who got in her car, they had to hear that cassette. She played it until it was worn out. Today, I can truly say she is healed.

Disappointed that she is gone but not discouraged because we know where she is.

Disappointed but Not Discouraged

Disappointed but Not Discouraged Notes

_____

_____

_____

_____

_____

_____

_____

_____

_____

_____

_____

_____

_____

_____

_____

_____

_____

Disappointed But Not Discouraged!!!

Uncle Walter Dixie Ballard

October 5, 1937 – August 13, 2019

Uncle Dule, as he was affectionally called, was married to my Mom's only sister (Aunt Jackie). He was a cool uncle. He always seemed to own nice things. A convertible sports car, when we were younger, was my favorite. When he saw me, he always called me "Gal."

When my dad passed in 2001, he stayed on my Mom to come and live with them before she would not have to live by herself. The ice storm was what brought Mom to their home.

Mom stayed off and on with Rick and me, but that did not solve the problems of loneliness or being cold all the time.

They had everything that my Mom was looking for. They had a wood stove and plenty of company all the time. Mom loved the woodstove and the company. Years were added to her life because they allowed her to come and stay with them.

Uncle Dule got sick with cancer, and my husband and I would go and pray with him and Aunt Jackie often. Members from our church, including Elder Carolyn Blue and Prophetess Virginia Hines, would also pray with them when things got a little heavy.

Cancer is not a joke. I am praying that one day, a cure will be found that will not entail chemo or radiation.

Before getting bedridden, he would come to the nursing home to visit Mom. I remember one of the times that he visited, he asked her when she was coming back home. She told him she didn't know.

Afterward, I explained to him that Mom would not return to their home. I also told him how much I appreciated everything he and Aunt Jackie did for Mom. It was because of them that her life was extended.

Cancer overtook Uncle Dule peacefully on August 13, 2019, while he was at home.

During his homegoing celebration, there were enough family members (nieces and nephews) to fill every spot on the program. His Pastor – Rev. Dr. Henry James Young, did the Eulogy. A poem entitled The Dash by Linda Ellis was included. That poem summed up his life.

"The Dash"

I read of a man who stood to speak at the funeral of a friend. He referred to the dates on his tombstone from the beginning to the end. He noted that first came the date of his birth and spoke of the following date with tears. But he said what mattered most of all was the dash between those years. For that dash represents all the time that he spent alive on earth. And now only those who loved him know what the little line is worth.

Disappointed but Not Discouraged

Disappointed but Not Discouraged Notes

_____
_____
_____
_____
_____
_____
_____
_____
_____
_____
_____
_____
_____
_____
_____
_____
_____
_____
_____
_____

Ministering to Mom

Four months before Mom passed, she had surgery to remove part of her cracked hip. The doctor said that was all he could do because she would not survive a total hip replacement. He was right because, after 30 minutes, all her vitals started to drop. After surgery, she was placed in Azalea Health and Rehab Center for rehab, then transferred to NorthChase Nursing Home for long-term nursing care. Uncle Dule came to see her and told her to hurry and get better so she could return home. That never happened.

Mom passed on May 24, 2018, after being in constant pain from the surgery. She would scream daily for the last four months of her life from the pain. I was by her bedside every day except one. That one day, my body shut down, and I could not go anymore.

When I would be with her, we would have some serious conversations. I sat myself down in church. I didn't pray for anyone. I did not preach, teach, or do anything pertaining to church. Mom became my ministry. She asked me, **"Sandus, what have I done that was so bad that the Lord is**

punishing me?" This was an awesome moment for me to share with her.

I actually shared my sermon that I ended up ministering at her Eulogy.

I shared with her the story of Job. I reminded her how Job lost everything, including his children. What folk did not realize is God was bragging about Job. Therefore, what you are going through, God is bragging on you.

These folks at this nursing home are amazed at how many people come to see you. They are amazed at how people talk about what a great person you are. God is Bragging on You. Even though when they turn you to change your diaper or the foot doctor comes and works on your feet, you always tell them thank you for not hurting you, even though they did. God is bragging on you. It seemed as if she felt better after that sermon.

In 2001, when Dad passed, Mom said, "Wayne did your Dad's funeral, and I want you to do mine." It was hard, but I got through it because I was......

Disappointed but Not Discouraged

Disappointed but Not Discouraged Notes

_____

_____

_____

_____

_____

_____

_____

_____

_____

_____

_____

_____

_____

_____

_____

_____

_____

_____

Disappointed But Not Discouraged!!!

Remembering Cousin Candie

On Wednesday, December 18, 2019, I cried. I cried because my cousin, Candie, was sent to hospice to end her battle with cancer. I cried because her son was there when I finally got there, and he was crying. Something about a man crying that gets to you: I cried because he was so lost.

Life is so short. Candie is only in her 70s. So young. She passed on **Thursday, December 26, 2019**, with family at her side. Again, I cried. Folk look at me and think I am so strong. Here I am in the midst of writing another book, this one entitled – **Disappointed but not discouraged**, talking about death and dying. Yet I find myself still crying after someone has died or battling cancer. I hate cancer.

Candie was that cousin that took me under her wings at an early age. I was not even old enough to go to school, but she would take me with her. She taught me how to ride my bike and so many other things.

After moving to Wilmington after getting married, we still kept in contact with each other. When I heard she was sick, I volunteered to transport her to her appointments at Duke Hospital in Durham, NC. We were there for each other.

Her death again has me **disappointed but not discouraged**.

Her husband, Harry Thomas, joined her on Friday, February 3, 2022. He was lost without her. He suffered from dementia and looked for Candie every day. They were married for 46 years.

Harry introduced me to my first husband; our oldest son, Ulric, was his godson.

He had an awesome homegoing as well.

Disappointed but not discouraged because Harry had dementia, but he never forgot who held him in HIS hands.

Disappointed but not Discouraged.

Disappointed but Not Discouraged Notes

_____

_____

_____

_____

_____

_____

_____

_____

_____

_____

_____

_____

_____

_____

_____

_____

_____

Disappointed But Not Discouraged!!!

Elder Hazel Hewitt Miller

Wednesday, December 25, 2019, I received a call from a relative asking me if I knew Hazel was in the hospital. I said I didn't know and would be praying for her. She said she was in room 1010. She said to call before you go to see her. I said wait a minute.

The 10th floor of the hospital is reserved for hospice patients. What are you saying? She said that Hazel has cancer. Lord No. I am numb at this point. Elder Hazel and Evangelist Florence Wheeler were sent by Apostles Theodore and Joyce Jones in 2002 to help us (Uplifting Faith Ministries, Inc.) get started with the ministry. What a blessing she was. Always so bubbly.

Today is Christmas Day, and I had dinner for over 20 guests. Hazel stayed in my spirit all day. Finally, when the final guest left, I told my husband I was going to the hospital to see Hazel and to Hospices to see Candy. He said he was going with me. Room 1010. Wow. Her Mom was there and recognized me right away. We embraced. Others were there as well. Melvin, her brother-in-law, Apostle Bryon Mckoy's wife, and a cousin from out of town were also there.

I sat near her Mom, and we talked. In the background, I could hear the death rattle, as the old folks called it. Memories. Memories. It was in 2018 when I heard that rattle from my mom. Little did I know that Hazel, my friend, would take her flight shortly after that. Again, I am numb. I got the call the next day that she passed. She had so many plans.

Elder Hazel and I had been friends from back in the day. We were both members of Life Changing Ministries, Inc. at the same time. She loved her pastors. We would ride to church together, bible study, and other services.

When the Lord called me into full-time ministry in January 2001, Apostles Theodore and Joyce I. Jones, as I stated earlier, sent her along with Evangelist Florence Wheeler to help us get started. They were allowed to stay with us for three (3) months, and then they had to return to their own church. She was a joy to be around. You could never have a dull day around her. Before they left, my husband, Deacon Ricky Henry Randolph, joined us. He later was ordained Elder and became the Pastor.

Disappointed that she is gone but not discouraged because I know without a shadow of doubt that Elder Hazel is with the Lord, telling Him daily that she loves Him. (her famous words to everyone)

Disappointed but not Discouraged.

Disappointed but Not Discouraged Notes

_____
_____
_____
_____
_____
_____
_____
_____
_____
_____
_____
_____
_____
_____
_____
_____
_____
_____
_____

Disappointed But Not Discouraged!!!

Cousin Lillian Mayfair Hayes
(DOD 1/12/2020)

...was affectionally called Mayfair by most of us. As far back as I can remember, she was always very independent. She had her own house, car, job, and money. She was a classy type of lady. Then she had a stroke, driving home from a funeral that she attended. The story is told that she got to the light on 3rd and Dawson Street and became confused. Someone saw her, and she allowed them to drive her home.

Her brother, James Jr., as we called him, convinced her to go to the ER, and she finally did. From that point, she never returned home.

She was placed in a nursing home, actually, the same nursing home that Bridget, my sister, was in. At least once a month, after being contacted by Pam, her daughter, I would go and do her nails. This would entail polishing both her hands and feet, greasing them down with oil, and praying over her. She noticed that I would keep coming and told me to call Terry, her son, and tell him to give me one hundred dollars ($100) out of her dresser drawer. That was one Mother's Day weekend, and I told her it was her

Mother's Day gift from me. She never offered again. I told her she did not owe me anything because she was good to my mother, Deaconess Louise Burns.

When I said that, she would tell me the story of her childhood. She said Sis Lizzy (my grandmother) would take children into her home, but it was Bay's (my mother) job to take care of them. Bay would get the big tub every Saturday night and wash us up. She would use the same water as well. She was forever grateful to her for that.

Her health started to fail. She even had a feeding tube. On Sunday, January 12, 2020, Pam called me to inform me that her Mom was in hospice, and they were not expecting her to make it. I got dressed and went out and stayed with her until she transitioned. Terry and his wife were there, and so was Ray and his wife. I immediately knew from previous experience that it would not be long. She had that death rattle bad. Once you hear it, usually the person dies the next day.

Terry was distraught and kept saying his mother would be ok. Then he looked at me and asked me what did I think. I am not even sure what I told him. He finally left because he could not stand to see her suffering.

Cousin Mayfair went home to be with the Lord shortly after Terry and Ray left.

Pam called the funeral home (Davis Funeral Home), and we left before they came. She made all the arrangements and asked me if I would do the Eulogy. I informed her that I would be honored to help, but the protocol was she had to contact the Pastor of the church (Myrtle Grove A.M.E.) first and make sure it was ok. She did, and I did the Eulogy of our cousin.

Outline of my message for her Eulogy

Celebration of Life for Lillian Mayfair Hayes

Pray
Acknowledgments
Special thanks

Facts – Cousin Mayfair preached her own funeral by the life that she led. Therefore, my job as the Eulogist is very easy because I am going to explain to each of you just what her life meant. Mom, Mommy, Mother, Grandma, Grandmother, Grammy, Sister, Cousin, Friend....

Her name - Lillian – innocence, purity, beauty

Mayfair – mind, child with intelligence

Other names – sassy, strong-willed, giver...

Holy Ghost

Scripture – Isaiah 41:10 (read)

Subject – From Independent to Dependent

Holy Ghost

Independent – not influenced or controlled by others in opinions, conduct, thinking, or acting for oneself.

Holy Ghost

At an early age, Cousin Mayfair's mother died. Independence was thrust on her like never before. But God had a plan.

Every occasion I visited with her, she told me about Sis. Lizzie and Bay.

They taught her the greatest dependence - the plan of salvation - **on the mourner's bench.**

A – accept the Lord Jesus as your personal Lord and Savior

B – You believe that Jesus died on the cross for you. Even if you were the only sinner, He still would have died for you.

C – Now confess that I am a sinner, and I want to be saved.

From Independent to Dependent

Then, she was taught **Psalm 23 under the weeping willow tree in the backyard**.

1 - The Lord is my shepherd: I shall not want.

2 - He maketh me to lie down in green pastures: he leadeth me beside the still waters.

3 - He restoreth my soul: he leadeth me in the paths of righteousness for his name's sake.

4 - Yea, though I walk through the valley of the shadow of death. I will fear no evil: for thou art with me; thy rod and thy staff they comfort me:

5 - Thou preparest a table before me in the presence of mine enemies; thou anointest my head with oil; my cup runneth over.

6 - Surely goodness and mercy shall follow me all the days of my life; and I will dwell in the house of the Lord for ever.

Holy Ghost

Dependent – to lean on someone/something to the point you can't function without their help.

Holy Ghost

Mother was gone, but now she had Jesus.
Isaiah 41:10 – Fear thou not; for I am with thee: be not dismayed; for I am thy God.

Holy Ghost

Independent – washed herself, clothed, made her own money, paid her own bills, and cared for her children, grandchildren, and others. She was taught and illustrated by her lifestyle to put your trust in the Lord.

Isaiah 41:10 - I will strengthen thee; yea I will help thee:

Independent

1) Biggest house on the block (share with others)

2) The smallest and best car, the VW

3) Biggest attitude of helping others

4) Always willing to give back

Holy Ghost

Twenty months ago, she had a stroke, and she became dependent upon others to bathe her, feed her, clothe her, pay her bills, and take care of her.

The stroke affected her right side, but you saw the effects on the left side.

Isaiah 41:10 – yea, I will uphold thee with the right hand of my righteousness.

Holy Ghost

Cousin Mayfair grabbed hold of God's unchanging hand and would not let go. Physical therapy could not break her bond with her Master and Savior.

From Independent to Dependent

Point #1 – Don't be dismayed

Point #2 – God will strengthen you

Point #3 – God will help you

Point #4 – God will uphold you with the right hand of his righteousness.

Conclusion – if you have a relationship with God like Cousin Mayfair, you can depend on Him to see you through any trial or tribulation.

Psalms 27:10 – When my father and my mother forsake me, then the Lord will take me up.

From Independent to Dependent

Sunday, January 12, around 9:15 p.m., Lillian Mayfair Hayes made a final choice to become totally dependent upon the Lord. She knew that Terry and Ray would not understand her decision, so she waited until they left. Then she took hold of the Lord's hand and said, "Ok, I am now ready to be totally dependent upon you."

Now I say to each of you, make sure you are leaning and depending on the Lord. If you don't know Him as your personal Savior, get to know Him Now!!!!

From Independent to Dependent

Again, I am disappointed that she is not here but not discouraged because I know where she is.

Disappointed but Not Discouraged Notes

_____
_____
_____
_____
_____
_____
_____
_____
_____
_____
_____
_____
_____
_____
_____
_____
_____
_____
_____

Disappointed But Not Discouraged!!!

Elder Tanya B. Millhouse - February 5, 2020

Elder Tanya B. Millhouse was not only a member of our church but also a personal friend. Our favorite thing to do together was shopping for purses at the outlet twice a year. Her nephew worked at the outlet, which entitled us to a 50% discount. There were other discounts as well, for which we sometimes ended up paying $5.00 (five dollars per purse). The outlet was Noella in Scottshill, North Carolina. The first year we went, everyone in our church got a purse. Because of her and her nephew, I got purses, carry-on bags, scarves, and many other things. On our last trip for their previous sale, Millhouse was so sick. She was faithful in wanting to go, and I felt terrible, but I needed that discount.

When she went home to be with the Lord, I was lost. In and out of the hospital, chemo and radiation for that awful disease called cancer.

I remember when she called me to inform me that she had cancer. She then went back to work. I had to pull off the road after her telling me this, and she returned to work. She was so strong. I felt my disappointment setting in. I spent as much time with her as I could, and then she took her wings.

My husband ministered the Eulogy, and I was the presider. Her other best friend, Cynthia, had remarks ending with Thank you for being my friend. Again, I am **Disappointed but not Discouraged!!!!**

Disappointed but Not Discouraged Notes

_____

_____

_____

_____

_____

_____

_____

_____

_____

_____

_____

_____

_____

_____

_____

_____

_____

_____

_____

Disappointed But Not Discouraged!!!

Cousin Derrick Terrell Ballard
- January 27, 1971 - May 21, 2020.

Derrick Ballard was my cousin. He was the last son of Aunt Jackie. She had been through so much. Her husband had just passed, and Derrick had a massive stroke.

I prayed like I had never prayed before. I begged the Lord to please Jesus, don't take him. His mom has just buried her husband, and no matter how strong she seemed on the outside, please, please, Lord, she can't take anymore. Well, he was in the hospital, not able to talk, speech was slugged, and looking confused. After four days, he was able to walk out of the hospital with no side effects. God performed that miracle. God did it.

Well, on May 21, 2020, in the middle of the pandemic, when no visitors were allowed, in the rehab part of the hospital, he had a massive heart attack and passed. We were told that all the staff present were upset. Aunt Jackie called me and told me where she was. When I went to the hospital, not to see Derrick but to find Aunt Jackie. They took me to Derrick's room. I was distraught. I told them I was looking for his mother because there was nothing that I could do for Derrick now. I found her in the front of the hospital. I took her with me or drove her car to mine. I can't remember which one I did. All I know is that Derrick passed nine months after his father.

Derrick was a volunteer fireman, among other things at the Navassa Fire Department. After the funeral, Mrs. Minnie Brown made a statement that I knew would end my book. She called his call number and said he answered his last call. That really tore me up. His work was completed. Here I am again, **Disappointed but not Discouraged**.

Disappointed but Not Discouraged Notes

_____

_____

_____

_____

_____

_____

_____

_____

_____

_____

_____

_____

_____

_____

_____

_____

_____

_____

_____

_____

Disappointed But Not Discouraged!!!

Apostle Patricia Ann Melvin
(3-5-1954 -9-14-2021)

On Tuesday, September 14, 2021, around 6:22 a.m., I received a text saying – good morning! My mom has taken her rest. I tried to call you. This was by far the worst text I could have gotten. It concerned my friend, our spiritual daughter – **Apostle Patricia Ann Melvin**. She had been in the hospital ICU unit for quite some time, BUT she had been there before. We (those who were sincerely praying for her) believed that she would return home, call me, and say, "Doc, when can you do my feet?" Well, according to this call, this will never happen.

I was disappointed but not discouraged that Doc (affectionally called by me) would not call for that last appointment. **Yes**, I know that she is no longer suffering. **Yes**, I know she is in a better place. Yes, I know all that and some more, **BUT** I am so disappointed. I was disappointed in the saints that had her dead several weeks ago, disappointed how that news spread like wildfire—disappointed because I will not get to do my friend's feet again—rubbing them with **2 Old Goats Ointment** to help with her other soreness. Disappointed because after rubbing them, I could see instant results.

Today, I got up. I got dressed and went swimming at the **YMCA**. I sent out a brief announcement to all of my contacts. From that point, I did not answer any phone calls. I could not talk about what I was feeling. I did not want to hurt anyone's feelings because, at this point, I am in **my feelings**. My eyes began to leak. At one point, it was like a faucet dripping and not stopping.

This was so hard to swallow. I began to think about all the things that we did together. It went as far back as our times together with the Samuel Irving Drama Troupe. Doc always got the part of the Praying Woman (even though it was drama, she made you feel what the praying woman was feeling) and one of the Brides of Christ. I always said that there is a thin line between drama and reality. Doc always crossed it, as well as myself.

Then, we both worked for New Hanover County. She was the first Black Woman to be the Assistant County Manager. One of the departments she covered was the Register of Deeds, where I worked. My boss and I got along well until she started allowing someone to whisper in her ear.

I experienced racism like none other. I was demoted from Administrative Assistant to Deputy I. Before all the racism came in full bloom, I was trained to work in all of the departments in the ROD office. I was able to relieve any employee at any given time. After being on vacation for three weeks and returning, the Lord always had me a step ahead of my enemies. I was 50 years old and had 20 years in the retirement system, so I decided to retire.

I filled out all the paperwork without telling my boss, whose plans were to fire me. After all the paperwork was in order then and only then, I informed her that I was retiring. I was supposed to retire on a Monday, but after talking to my next-door neighbor on that Friday, on my way to work, he said why go back, go to lunch, and don't go back. **WOW**.

After checking with HR, That was what I did to ensure it would not hurt my retirement. When the boss got back to work on Monday, I was gone. She contacted Dr. Melvin and asked her what could she do to me. Dr. Melvin had a way of responding to you with your own question to make you hear yourself, and you would feel stupid. Dr. Melvin reminded her that I had retired. I was gone. There is nothing that she could do to me. I was no longer her problem, as she called me. Dr. Melvin always had my back.

Disappointed But Not Discouraged.

A few years later, the Lord elevated Doc again. She became the **Senior Ambassador of the International Embassy of Holiness**. She loved her family and her church family as well. She always had their backs. She knew protocol. She made an appointment with us and asked if we would be her

Spiritual Coverings. She told us that she was starting a church. We were honored. She became our **"Baby Girl."** Even though others joined our ministry, she was always the **"Baby Girl."** She had a heart of gold. She made sure all of the children under her leadership were properly trained. She even paid for some of them to attend our Bread of Life College. Embassy, she had your backs. Even when she started to get sick, we were helping her train her leaders.

Dr. Melvin was the speaker at one of the Association of Covenant Churches conventions. Her sermon was – There's A Shift.
As she was ministering, the Lord gave me a song in reference to her message. (Tune of There's a Leak in this Old Building)

<u>There's A Shift</u>

There's a shift in this old building
Because my feet have got to move,
My feet have got to move,
My feet have got to move.
There's a shift in this old building
Because my feet have got to move
Another level/ is in/ my shifting.

Sometimes, folk won't understand
Because my feet have got to move,
My feet have got to move
My feet have got to move.
Sometimes, folk won't understand
Because my feet have got to move

Another levelll/ is in/ my shifting.

Today, I'm letting go.
Because my feet have got to move,

My feet have got to move,
My feet have got to move.
Today, I'm letting go.
Because my feet have got to move,
Another levelll/ is in/ my shifting.

I'm moving forward now.
Because my feet have got to move,
My feet have got to move,
My feet have got to move,
I'm moving forward now
Because my feet have got to move,
Another levelll/ is in/ my shifting.

<u>Written by</u>

Apostle Sandra B. Randolph 4-13-2019

Disappointed But Not Discouraged.

In 2018, she was elevated again to **Apostle Patricia Ann Melvin**.

From that point on, she started coming to us for one-on-one training, **BUT** she always had her side-kick, **Elder Angie**, with her. We would minister to her and build her back up after being torn down. The old saying, sticks and stones may break my bones, but names will never hurt me. This is **NOT** true. Words do hurt. She would always leave revived and ready to go back to the battlefield.

Disappointed But Not Discouraged.

Thank you, Shi, for allowing me this time to write this last chapter in my book.

You see.... We are disappointed today because she didn't keep her last appointment with us, But Not Discouraged because we know that she is in better hands with the Father.

My husband then did the spiritual word for others to take with them.

Scripture –John 2:1-5

Subject – Whatsoever She Said to You, Do It!!

Church, Family, Friends

Point #1 – Remember her prayers – (Luke 22:32)

Point #2 – Remember her words that she gave to you – (Proverbs 4:22)

Point #3 – Recant the assignment that she gave you.

Whatsoever She Said to You, Do It!!

Conclusion - John 15:7-8

He stated that we need to get on praying knees and seek the face of God. **Whatsoever She Said to You, Do It!!**

Last month, the Lord spoke to me and instructed me that Apostle Patricia Ann Melvin's life and death would be the closing of this book. There is nothing left to say on this subject.-

Disappointed But Not Discouraged....

Disappointed but Not Discouraged Notes

_____

_____

_____

_____

_____

_____

_____

_____

_____

_____

_____

_____

_____

_____

_____

_____

_____

_____

_____

_____

About the Author

Dr. Sandra Burns Randolph, is the daughter of the late Deacon Alfred and Deaconess Louise I. Burns, who was educated in the public schools of Brunswick County, North Carolina, and furthered her education by attending Fayetteville State University, Fayetteville, North Carolina, Miller-Motte Business College, Wilmington, North Carolina, Florida Theological College, Fayetteville, North Carolina (satellite campus), Bread of Life Institute, Whiteville, North Carolina and Wilmington, North Carolina. Dr. Randolph has a Doctorate in Divinity, Doctorate in Ministry and a Doctorate in Theology and currently is the Dean of School at the Bread of Life Institute, Wilmington, North Carolina campus.

Dr. Randolph is married to Dr. Ricky Henry Randolph. Together they serve as Apostles with five churches under their leadership, with Uplifting Faith Ministries, Inc. being the headquarters, located in Wilmington, North Carolina.

Together they have four sons and thirteen grandchildren. Dr. Randolph's motto is – "I want to leave a place better than I found it."

www.ingramcontent.com/pod-product-compliance
Lightning Source LLC
Chambersburg PA
CBHW071240020426

42333CB00015B/1561